The Philosophy of Unity in the Writings of Fazlur Rahman Ansari

Ahsan Academy of Research
(Springs, South Africa)

Muhammad Fazlur Rahman Ansari Series

1

The Philosophy of Unity in the Writings of Fazlur Rahman Ansari

Abdul Kader Choughley

Tawasul International
Centre for Publishing, Research and Dialogue

First Published 2024

ISBN : 978-93-88928-64-9
Abdul Kader Choughley

Ahsan Academy of Research
(Springs, South Africa)
ahsan@worldonline.co.za

Published by
Tawasul International
Centre for Publishing, Research and Dialogue, Rome, Italy

CONTENTS

THE PHILOSOPHY OF UNITY IN THE WRITINGS OF FAZLUR RAHMAN ANSARI

Abdul Kader Choughley

INTRODUCTION

An eminent scholar, Dr Muhammad Fazlur Rahman Ansari (d. 1974) made singular contributions to Islamic resurgence in the twentieth century. He excelled in Islamic and modern learning by virtue of his extensive studies in these respective fields. He taught comparative religion, moral philosophy and Islamic studies at the University of Karachi. Likewise, he established the Aleemiyah Institute of Islamic Studies - a premier seat of Islamic learning.

Ansari's seminal study, *The Qur'ānic Foundations and Structure of Muslim Society* (hereafter *The Qur'ānic Foundations*) encompasses the ethical teachings of the sacred text in a contemporary setting. His other writings and lectures bring to the fore his contributions to *tabligh* and contemporary Islamic thought.

PHIILOSOPHY OF UNITY

The concept of unity (*tawhid*) according to Ansari "[is] and all-pervading principle which governs all the fundamental domains of human faith and action."[1] In his discussion about man's relation with the universe, Ansari makes an important observation:

> What then should be our attitude towards our material environment? Should it consist in renouncing the world and repressing our physical desires? No. Islam says nothing of the kind. Instead of recognising antagonism between the moral and physical existence of man, it emphasises the co-existence

---

[1] Ansari, *The Qur'ānic Foundation and Structure of Muslim Society*, vol. 1 (Karachi, 2012), 173.

of these two aspects as the natural basis of life. It maintains that our earthly sojourn is a positive factor in the Divine scheme of creation and a necessary stage in the evolution of our soul- life. Consequently, it seeks the affirmation of the spiritual self in man, not in renouncing the world of matter, but in the active endeavour to master it with a view to discover a basis for a realistic regulation of life.

This realistic attitude of Islam may not, however, be identified with that of the modern West. The latter ignores our spiritual existence altogether and regards our earthly career as an end-in-itself, and that in a way which amounts to worship. Islam, on the other hand, conceives it not as an end but as a means to a higher spiritual end.

And what is that higher goal? It is submission to the Will of Allah and seeking His pleasure, as the Qur'ān says:

Say: Verily, my worship and my sacrifice and my living and my dying are Jor Allah, Lord of the Worlds, Who has no partner. (6: 63)[2]

According to Ansari, the Qur'ān promotes an integrated approach which harmonises man's relationship with worldly and other-worldly pursuits. Therefore, *tawhid* must be understood in a broader sense rather than the narrowly defined interpretation of beliefs (`aqā'id).

There are at least twenty one linkages to *tawhid* which fall within the purview of the Qur'ānic dimensions of this concept. These may be compared to various strands that are woven to form a beautiful tapestry. Similarly, the strands of *tawhid* are interwoven as explained in numerous verses (āyāt) of the Qur'ān.

We will now attempt to delineate sone of the salient features that characterise the philosophy of unity.

---

[2] Ansari, *Foundations of Faith* (Karachi, 1992), 49-50.

UNITY OF ALLAH

The Qur'ānic declaration of life is grounded in the purest monotheism - the doctrine in the Unity of Allah. *Tawhid* is the basis of the philosophy of life in Islam. Allah is One (*ahad*) and has no partner in godhead. The word thus emphatically conveys the meaning that Allah is One, the indivisible; He who has no partner to share in his lordship, nor in His essence or His attributes.[3] Belief in this attribute demands that man shows total and unconditional loyalty and devotion to Him. In other words, *tawhid* shuts out all forms of polytheism (*shirk*) that are prevalent in many religions like Hinduism. It is only Islam that has presented unalloyed *tawhid* in both belief and practice. As such it emancipates man "from every cosmic and earthly bondage and elevates him to the highest pinnacle of glory."[4]

UNITY OF THE UNIVERSE

Ansari states clearly that the universe has come into existence through creation, and Allah alone is the Creator. Therefore, there exists a unity of purpose in its existence - a reign of law and moral order that governs the universe. As opposed to scientific theories that postulate that the origin of the universe occurred by chance and therefore inherently possess the elements of chaos, the Qur'ān refers to it as a cosmos. This distinction is necessary to show how human life becomes meaningful within a cosmic order.

Again, the Qur'ān emphasises the emergence of the cosmos as an evolutionary creation through the Absolute Will of Allah. By the same token, Islam does not consider the universe as composed of two self-existing and conflicting entities. It conceives all life as a unity because it proceeds from the Divine Oneness (*tawhid*). In addition to the principle of harmony, Islam emphasises the purposive nature of all existence, whether spiritual or physical. Thus, Allah says in the

---

[3] A detailed commentary of *Surah al-Ikhlās* encapsulating *tawhid* appears in Daryabadi's *Tafsir-ul-Qur'ān* (Lucknow, 1983), vol. 4, 540-1.

[4] Ansari, *The Qur'ānic Foundations*, vol. 1, 173.

Qur'ān:

> *We have not created the heavens and the earth and whatever is between them in sport. We have not created them but for a serious end: but the greater part of them understand not.* (44: 38-9)

Ansari observes:

> Thus our earthly surroundings are not a meaningless projection of the play of blind forces - a mere empty shell with no content. The tiniest particle of sand, the smallest drop of water, the frailest rose-leaf is full of meaning and music, and functions under a definite and well-planned Divine scheme.[5]

Touching on doctrinal issues in respect of the relation of Allah with the cosmos, Ansari emphasises the creed of the *Ahl al-Sunnah wa'l-Jamā'ah*[6] known as Sunnis. They emphasise the teachings of the Qur'ān n and the sunnah of the Holy Prophet (pbuh) along with the collective judgement (*ijmā'*) of the *Sahābah*, Companions of the Holy Prophet (pbuh). According to the Qur'ān, Allah is Eternal and Absolute and the cosmos is transient and relative. It has originated by the will of the Absolute and sustained by the Absolute. In other words, the cosmos being relative has no existence of its own. This philosophical doctrine[7] is integral to the Sunni creed (*'aqidah*).

The universe being a whole, all forms of life therefore reflect an organic unity. With respect to mankind, it is distinguished from other forms of life because it functions within the framework of a personality. Man undergoes an evolutionary process[8] in terms of his earthly life and his life after death. Therefore, these phases are a projection of unity.

---

[5] Ansari, *Foundations of Faith*, 48.

[6] For a detailed discussion about the *Ahl-al-Sunnah*, see Abdur Rahman Doi, "Sunnism" *in Islamic Spirituality* (New York, 1992), vol. 1.

[7] The orthodox theology (*kalām*) developed by its two exponents, Al-Ash`ari and Maturidi is extensively covered in M.M. Sharif, *A History of Muslim Philosophy*, vol.1 (Karachi, 1983), 220-273. Cf. Abu Hanifah's *Al-Fiqh Al-Akbar Expiained* (Santa Barbara, 2007).

[8] Ansari, *The Qur'ānic Foundations*, vol. 1, 177.

UNITY OF KNOWLEDGE

The organic unity in general is a manifestation of Allah's divine will. Proceeding from the universe which is a projection of unity, Ansari clearly states that knowledge too should be vigorously pursued in terms of unity. In his major writings and lectures, he has consistently advanced the cause of knowledge which rejects the division of 'religious' and 'secular'. In fact, the poet of the East, Iqbal (d. 1938) has tersely remarked:

Talk of modern and ancient is the sign of narrowness of vision.

It is the *iqrā* framework - the message for knowledge (`*ilm*) that changed the course of history. The Muslims' role in harnessing knowledge is emphasised. Likewise, the message given to Muslims is that the function of this *ummah* will be "[to] unearth all the treasures of knowledge that are buried in the different civilisations of the world: to preserve, to classify and to rectify all the different types of knowledge and advance the course of knowledge."[9]

Furthermore, Ansari contends that the dichotomous educational system has created a cleavage in the mindset of the *ummah* with the result that they continue to harbour the illusion of the separation of knowledge. By contrast, Islamic civilisation during its heydays offered a different picture to what we witness today. Ansari's comments are illustrative:

> Now just as Islam does not base its conception of worship on the separation of the religious from the secular, similarly, in its concept of education, it does not exclude "secular" knowledge from the curriculum of "religious" studies in the manner in which the one-sided religions and cultures of the world do it. This is the reason why, during the age of glory of the Islamic civilisation, the educational system of the Muslim world was unitary, being based on the fundamental Islamic

---

[9] Yasien Mohamed, *Isiam to the Modern Mind* (Cape, 2006), 188.

principle of *tawhid*. In that system, theological sciences were taught in conjunction with all other so-called "secular" subjects, which included natural sciences, mathematics, philosophy, etc. The result was that every Muslim scholar of that age used to be a comprehensive scholar. Again, the formal system of examinations and award of formal certificates which is prevalent today was not in vogue at that time. Hence, none could obtain a certificate without genuinely acquiring the necessary knowledge and the requisite intellectual and spiritual discipline. Overall, everyone got an individual certificate in accordance with the actual intellectual stature he had acquired and this fixed his place in society. Moreover, spiritual discipline (*tazkiyah*) and character-building (*tarbiyah*) also formed a vital part of education side by side with academic attainments, and thus aptitude, labour and piety, all were fully co-ordinated, harmonised and rewarded.[10]

It was the mission of Islam that projected a challenge to the rest of the world. As such Muslim became pioneers in all fields of knowledge and synthesised "moral standards and spiritual values." Hardly surprising, therefore, was the spiritualising culture of Islam that left indelible imprints on the lives of nations who accepted Islam.

Ansari maintains that it is a correct understanding of man's role as a *khalifah* (custodian) that determines the outcome of integrated knowledge. This is borne out by the following comments which draw a comparison between the Islamic perspectives and Western attributes to knowledge:

Man is, by himself, not the origin or fountainhead of knowledge. He is simply the deputy or agent to actualise the Will of Allah on this earth. The most tragic and dangerous turn in the history of knowledge, or rather that of humanity, occurred when man forgot this basic fact that he is only an agent or representative of Allah, the Lord of the Worlds. He has been

---

[10] Mahdie Kriel, *Islamic Intellectual Revival of the Modern Mind* (Cape Town, 2011), 96-7.

given the charge of the world but not its ownership. He has not the right to use the resources found over and within this earth according to his wish or caprice or for the promotion of his limited national, ethnic, tribal or racial benefit, nor for achieving political and personal domination over others. It was the most dangerous moment in human history when mankind began to pursue knowledge along this disastrous course. Only a realisation that man is not the Lord or Master of the world but simply a vicegerent and deputy can keep him on the right path. Awareness of this basic fact alone can help him to act as a functionary, lieutenant, or second-in-command instead of an independent owner or master of the world.[11]

In terms of the scope and functions of knowledge, it is the Qur'ān that "charted a new course for the pursuers of science". In fact, the scientific quest, according to Ansari, completes the religious quest and forms part of *'ibādah*. The following *āyāh* reveals the progression of scientific discoveries in relation to the miraculous features of the Qur'ān:

In the time to come We (God) will show them (i.e., human beings) Our Signs in remote regions (of the universe) and in their (own) selves, until it becomes manifest to them that this (i.e. the Qur'ān) is the Truth... (41:53)[12]

UNITY OF FAITH AND REASON

The time-honoured separation between faith and reason was glaringly present in the Christian West at the period when Islamic civilisation projected its 'unitary dimension'. In other words, there was no worldly or other-wordly function of knowledge. It would be difficult to visualise the revolutionary nature of the fusion between faith and reason without tracing its links to the first Qur'ānic revelation: *iqrā*.

A point to be considered is that this twin concept was given tangible expression during its evolutionary phases in Islamic history. It was,

---

[11] Nadwi, *Islam and Knowledge* (Oxford, 1992), 9.
[12] The translation of the āyāh is paraphrased by Ansari.

therefore, not an isolated event; rather it created a rich legacy through which mankind benefitted immensely. Ansari says:

> A brief analysis of the first revelation deserves mention. First, the emphasis of the pursuit of knowledge forms the cornerstone of Islamic civilisation. Second, reference is made to the Lord of the universe who brought man into existence from a world of non-entity. Third, faith is interlinked with knowledge. In these verses, the psychology for the quest and promotion of knowledge through the pen (*qalam*) is articulated.[13]

This is further explained by Ansari: faith and reason have also to go together to function in unity. Faith without reason lands human being in superstition. Reason without faith deprives humanity of the highest values.[14]

In a similar vein, divine guidance (*wahy*) contains the basic truth for mankind. There is no contradiction between religion and scientific approach to truth which are complementary and has a single purpose of promoting unity in all facets of life.[15]

Truth, according to Ansari, permeates the spirit of enquiry. While maintaining a healthy balance between worldly and other-worldly pursuits, it consistently seeks to advance the inner dimensions of spirituality that are in stark contrast to the West's outlook to life. Seyyed Hossein Nasr has cogently demonstrated the West's failure to shore up spiritual gains through its unrestricted progress in technology and science.[16] It does not possess the redeeming qualities of a 'Sacred Law' that creates checks and balances in the pursuit of material needs.

As a result, the West or any community that deviates from the

---

[13] The struggle between the Church and knowledge in Christendom is too well-known. The American writer, W.H. Draper has documented this confrontation in his famous book, *History of the Conflict between Religion and Science* (1874).

[14] Ansari, *The Holy Prophet (SAW)'s Contribution to Knowledge* (Karachi, n.d.), 2. The article was an extempore lecture delivered at St. Patrick's college in 1972 and contains seminal ideas which he developed in *The Qur'ānic Foundations.*

[15] Ansari, *The Qur'ānic Foundations,* vol. 1, 178.

[16] Seyyed Hossein Nasr, *The Spiritual Crisis in Modern Man* (London, 1990), 134.

trajectory of *tawhid* cannot be in harmony or equilibrium with spiritual life, and ultimately with the source and origin of all things.[17]

This view is supported by Ansari in his critique about the West's apathy to matters of the heart.

A vital point of difference between the spirit of modern West and the spirit of Islam may however be emphasised again. While the modern West has employed science mostly for the satisfaction of its craving after power and pleasure, Islam seeks in the scientific inquiry a means to the service of humanity and spiritual elevation.[18]

UNITY OF RELIGION

The thematic significance of unity in relation to Allah and humanity reinforces the idea that religion has to be unitary in purpose. In other words, religion which is designated as Islam has not been confined to specific groups but rather mankind has been blessed with it during the course of human history. Divine guidance could not have been different for different communities nor could the message of *tawhid* meant something else to them. Like truth, divine revelation is universal. It is only the Qur'ānic revelation that offers a clear and coherent message about the unity of religion. Therefore, divine guidance, according to Ansari is derived from the same fundamentals and at the same time evolutionary in response to the development of human culture. Ansari says:

> Divine Guidance, according to Islam, has been universal. Adam was the first man and also the first Prophet of Allah. After him guidance continued to come from Allah to all the communities and countries of the world. The Holy Qur'ān says: *"Every people had a guide."* This guidance was fundamentally the same wherever it came, because it came from the one Allah and it came to the same humanity. Though the same in its fundamentals, it was at the same time evolutionary, expanding and developing in scope. As the various human

---

[17] Ibid., 136.
[18] Ansari, *Islam and Christianity in the Modern World,* 210-11.

communities progressed from a lower stage of culture and civilisation to a higher one, until when humanity reached maturity, it was finalised and perfected in the divine guidance given in the form of the Holy Qur'ān to the Holy Prophet (pbuh) who is the last and the greatest Messenger of Allah. As regards the Holy Qur'ān, it is not only the last Book of Allah but also the only one which exists without any interpolation and change up to this day.[19]

Abul Kalam Azad (d. 1958), the noted commentator of the Qur'ān, has made an incisive analysis of divine guidance:

The divine truth, says the Qur'ān, is a universal gift from Allah. It is not exclusive to any race or any people or religious group. Also, it is not exclusively delivered in any particular language. You have created for yourselves national, geographical and racial boundaries. But you cannot so divide the divine truth. That truth bears no national stamp, nor professes any racial or geographical loyalties or group affiliations. Like the sun created by Allah, it shines in every corner of the globe, and shines equally well on every one. If you care to have it, do not search for it in any particular corner. It is noticeable everywhere and has found expression in every age. Do not worship your communities, homelands, languages or your group formations. You should worship only Allah and respect this universal truth.[20]

In sum, it is the Qur'ān that sets the benchmark for interpreting and validating the previous teachings given to past communities. Its universal message bears unmissable imprints of guiding mankind towards truth in all its manifestations. Ansari's comments are pertinent in this regard:

Divine revelation provides the venue of appeal to the

---

[19] Ansari, *Foundations of Faith*, 26.
[20] Abul Kalam Azad, *Tarjuman al-Qurān*, vol. 1. Translated into English by Syed Abdul Latif (Lahore, n.d.), 172.

religions of the world for casting off the shells of later accretions, perversions and distortions brought into existence by human ignorance, ingenuity or vested interests, and returning to the original message in the light of reason and with the assistance of the Qur'ānic revelation and paving the way to the unity of mankind.[21]

UNITY OF MANKIND

The historic declaration of the unity of mankind is forcefully explained in the following ayah:

> *O mankind! We created Jor you a single (pair) of male and female, and made you into nations and tribes, that you may know each other. Certainly, the most honoured of you in the sight of Allah is the most righteous of you... (49:13)*

Muhammad Hashim Kamali maintains that the above āyāh clarifies the bond of unity for mankind:

> It is explicit to the unity of origin; and equality in creation of the entire human race. Their descent from a common ancestor places all in a position where they bear a central obligation towards one another...[22]

Thus, the Islamic concept of creating an egalitarian society was free from class struggle or confrontation for equality and justice. Likewise, the social revolution it brought about has been a source of inspiration for the charter of human equality. It has served as a model for individuals and organisations seeking to translate this ideal into reality.[23]

The Holy Prophet (pbuh) simultaneously announced the concept of human equality:

---

[21] Ansari, *The Qur'ānic Foundations*, vol. 1, 179.

[22] Mohammad Hashim Kamali, *Freedom, Equality and Justice in Islam* (Cambridge, 2010), 51.

[23] Ibid., 47

O Mankind, Your God is One and you have one father. You are all progeny of Adam, and Adam was made of clay. There is no doubt that the noblest among you, in the sight of Allah, is the one who is best in conduct. No Arab has any preference over a non-Arab over non-Arab over an Arab except by his piety.[24]

This twin declaration of the unity of God and mankind are the natural foundations on which the structure of peace and progress, equally and justice, tolerance and co-operation between different people and nations is built.

A corollary to the unity of mankind is the Qur'ānic proclamation of human dignity. Before the prophethood of the holy Prophet (pbuh), human dignity had reached its lowest ebb. Human lives were sacrificed at the altar of superstitious rituals, mythological traditions and individual egoism.[25] This gloomy spectacle was not confined to Arabia; other civilisations possessing a 'high culture' considered human dignity as inconsequential.

The deplorable events before the advent of Islam underpinned the importance of reasserting human dignity.[26] Overall, it was the clarion call of the Qur'ān which eradicated all vestiges of racial and tribal prejudices termed as Days of Ignorance (*jāhiliyah*) and restored the dignity of man that is unparalleled in human history.

PRINCIPLE OF UNITY IN RESPECT OF THE SEXES

The revolutionary tenor of the Qur'ānic verses and the teachings of the Holy Prophet (pbuh) in terms of women's rights reaffirmed

---

[24] *Kanz ai-'Ammāl.*

[25] Refer to Gibbon's *The Fall of the Roman Empire* which documents the gross violation of human dignity by the Roman emperors.

[26] Ansari, *Islamic Intellectual Revival of the Modern Mind,* 37-45. Cf. Ansari, *Muhammad The Glory of the Ages* (Karachi, 2016). Several important publications of Ansari have been edited by the erudite scholar, Dr Umair Mahmood Siddiqui.

the Islamic declaration of human rights. Although the basic functions of man and woman differ they stand out as complementarity and therefore are united in the bond of humanity. Ansari has elaborated the unity of the sexes in these words:

> The first principle of a man's life is that all human beings (man and woman) should have their dealings on the principle of goodwill and understanding of one another.

Do not forget magnanimity in your dealings with one another. (8:1)

Not only justice and maintenance of peace in a healthy society, but magnanimity and grace are to be exercised towards those who are weaker than us, or placed in our charge. This is the universal law, the other principle is:

[Who] conduct their affairs by mutual consultation. (42:38)

Muslims are those who pursue all their dealings on the basis of mutual consultation on and not in the spirit of dictators.[27]

UNITY IN BASIC SOCIAL LIFE

In its promotion of an ideal society, the Holy Qur'ān makes an unequivocal declaration about the prevailing social inequalities facing mankind. Two strands of social stigma hindered the progress of an ideal society. First, the priestly class morphed into an institutionalised religious phenomenon and dictated devotional prayers to appease the phalanx of gods. Hinduism represented this trend. Second, even monotheistic religions like Judaism and Christianity could not free themselves from the shackles of superstition with the result that individuals were exposed to a multitude of deities to pray to.

Societal distinctions compounded by the ubiquitous priesthood

---

[27] *Islam to the Modern Mind*, 215-6. Translations of *āyāt* in the text are based on Ansari's interpretations and are therefore not literal meanings.

were an anathema to the Islamic social order. In several ayat of the Holy Qur'ān, a new value system was created in which the virtues of goodness and spiritual refinement were emphasised. Ansari's incisive remark about the Qur'ānic revolution is revealing:

> Negatively, through the abolition of the institution of priesthood and positively, through the creation of a classless, casteless and non- racial society, the Holy Qur'ān has sounded the death-knell to all such evil distinctions.[28]

Islamic ideals were translated into positive action. Social responsibility formed the basis of the Islamic society and moral conscience was harnessed as a religious obligation. It would be no exaggeration to say that the Holy Prophet's moulded his *Sahābah* to be the true representatives of the Islamic society,[29] which had been established in Madinah.

The *Sahābah* were the true embodiment of the social conscience, preservers and custodians of the moral order in Allah's universe. Any attempts to marginalise their importance or dislodge their singular contributions in building a vibrant Muslim community are indeed lamentable. Their exceptional devotion to Islamic cause can be gauged from their scrupulous efforts to preserve the Qur'ān in its pristine form.[30]

UNITY IN TERMS OF POLITICS

In Islam the state is based on *tawhid*; therefore, rule and sovereignty are in the hands of Allah alone. *Tawhid* rejects the idea that the Greek philosophers could formulate values associated with an ideal state.[31] In a similar vein, the nineteenth and twentieth century thinkers like Hegel idolised the state with unfettered powers.

---

[28] Ansari, *The Qur'ānic Foundations*, vol. 1, 182.

[29] The multivolume *Muhammad: Encyclopedia of Seerah* (London, 1988) also focuses on distinctive features of the Islamic society.

[30] Ansari, *The Qur'ānic Foundations,* vol. i, 88-90.

[31] See Ernest Barker, *Greek Political Theory: Plato and His Predecessor* (London, 1918).

Again, the Marxist state[32] through its 'iron regimentation' reduced the citizens as mere automatons. Overall, the politburo was invested with powers to dictate the political destiny of the citizens. This policy is countered by Ansari in his critical examination of the Communist challenge to Islam. He describes the Communist propaganda as a 'sunshine of illusions' that attracts the masses under deceptive masks. A godless ideology, Communism has made the trappings of materialism appealing. Hence, it remains in perpetual conflict with the perfect social order of Islam.[33] For example, accountability to the supremacy of the Law was ingrained in the lives of the *Sahābah* who assumed positions of leadership. In his augural address by the first Caliph of Islam, Abubakr said: "Obey me as long as I obey Allah and His Messenger. However, if I deviate from obedience to Allah and His Messenger, obedience to me remains binding on you no more."[34]

It was the democratic spirit of Islam that cut the roots of autocratic rule. For this reason, dictatorship in the form of imperial rule or the divine rights of kings which trampled human rights faced formidable challenges by the revolutionary concept of the Islamic state. There were no parallel institutions like the 'Church' and the 'State' perpetuating a great divide between the physical, moral and spiritual interests of its citizens. Islam wants to maintain an integrated outlook in respect of the citizens' diverse needs.

The political system conceived by Islam bore the hallmarks of altruism. It drew a distinction between self-interest and sacrifice. As a result, no claims to hereditary entitlements were discernible in the formative period of Islamic history.

UNITY IN TERMS OF ECONOMICS

Ansari provides clear outlines about the Islamic formulation of economics. The basis of this institution is the concept of values which is derived from the fundamental human rights charter.

---

[32] Ansari's critique of Marxism is summarised in his *Islam versus Marxism* (Karachi, 1982).

[33] Ansari, *Communist Challenge to Islam* (Karachi, 2018), 221-2.

[34] Ansari, *The Qur'ānic Foundations,* vol. 1, 182-3.

Freedom and equality[35] form the bedrock of economics. However, intrinsic to these values is the harmonious blending which Islam advocates. The history of Capitalism and Socialism illustrates the failure of these systems in achieving a just economic order except through the adoption of justice (*'adālah*).[36] This universal concept aligns freedom and equality in the economic sphere and creates the element of equilibrium as a guiding factor. Thus, a synthesis emerges which makes it possible "to establish a welfare society which will formulate on the principles, not of class war or of exploitation by the moneyed class but of love, harmony, human fellowship which will ensure a just distribution of wealth on the basis of just reward for labour, talent and achievement that will guarantee every citizen the basic needs of life."[37] Umar Chapra has encapsulated the function of the economic order in these words:

> Since human beings are the *khalifah* of Allah, they are subservient to none but Him. Serfdom of any kind, irrespective of whether it is social, political or economic, is, therefore, alien to the teachings of Islam. The Qur'ān states that one of the primary objectives of the Prophet Muhammad (pbuh) is to release mankind from the burdens and chains that have been imposed upon them (7:157). Accordingly, no one, not even the state, has the right to abrogate this freedom and to subject human life to any kind of bondage or regimentation. It is this teaching which prompted 'Umar, the second Caliph, to ask: "Since when have you enslaved people although they were given birth as free individuals by their mothers?"[38]

The ideal economic order Islam embraces diversification of activity. Thus, differentiated groups contribute meaningfully to sustainable activities based on their diverse skills, quality of labour

---

[35] A detailed discussion on the concept of freedom and equality appears in *Kamali, Freedom, Equality and Justice in Islam* (Cambridge, 2002), 1-102.

[36] In Islam the integrated vision of the citizens' diverse needs were given prominence. See Ansari, *Communist Challenge to Islam*, 243-8. Cf. Ansari, *The Qur'ānic Foundations*, vol.1 161-2.

[37] Ansari, *The Qur'ānic Foundations*, vol. i, 185.

[38] Muhammad Umer Chapra, *Islam and the Economic Challenge* (Leicester, 1992), 208.

and creative talents.

According to Ansari, there exists a variation in the economic order envisaged by Islam. This is natural in view of the inherent differing capabilities of mankind. It is, however, exploitation and injustice that are a blight to it progress. The Qur'ān advocates a unifying factor that takes into account values that challenge capitalistic societies, and instead establishes a welfare society based on truth, love and justice. This in essence is the principle of *human unity*.[39]

PRINCIPLE OF UNITY AS THE BASIS OF CULTURE

The bipolar vision of 'worldly' and 'other worldly' pursuits is vehemently rejected by Islam. The Qur'ān instead declares that human fulfilment includes the good and positive values of both worlds. This is clearly explained in the sacred text:

... Our Lord give us good in this world and in the hereafter and save us from the torment of the Fire. (2: 201)

For Ansari the blossoming of Islamic culture[40] is unprecedented in history. It represents the best ideals for human progress and has immensely influenced other civilisations that had come into contact with its glorious legacy. Varied cultures were absorbed into its cosmopolitan outlook solely on the basis of unity. It was the touchstone for all human endeavours. Thus, Islamic culture was free from the constraints of rigidity and formalism. Additionally, it created a locus for creative intellectual activity. Sadly, Muslim decline set in when the unifying structure of Islamic civilisation was discarded.

UNITY IN TERMS OF THE 'IDEAL OF A SINGLE GOAL'

The diversity of activity over the centuries (in particular early nineteenth and twentieth century) had created a phenomenon of

---

[39] Ansari, *The Qur'ānic Foundations,* vol. 1, 187.

[40] For an overview about the grandeur of Islamic culture, see Muzaffar Iqbal, *The Making of Islamic Civilisation.* Cf. Ansari, *The Qur'ānic Foundations* vol.1, 219-43.

ideological systems that distorted the basic goal in life. Socialism is representative of this trend. Like other man-made ideological institutions, it believes in the physical world alone which Ansari terms a 'sensate culture'.[41] In other words, these systems transform diverse human yearnings into a philosophy.[42] It is obvious that such an attitude militates against the **integrated** (emphasis added) system of Islam which provides the only guidance to save mankind from disaster. This worldview is natural because Allah has created all human beings and with a plan and purpose: *khilafah*. Ansari says:

> What is the purpose of human life but to realise the potential of *khalifat Allah:* to follow the straight path and not to deviate from it. This is possible through *tawfiq* (divine assistance) from Allah and through His mercy. When man actualises his function as *khalifat Allah* he becomes the master over himself and the environment. In order to achieve this, he must conquer his lower self (*nafs*), which is the first level of the conquest of the self, and is the starting point for mastery over all else.
>
> The second level is the conquest of the environment. Because the human being lives in a social order, the maintenance of the purity of the individual's life is possible only if his environment is also pure. Thus every human being has to struggle individually and collectively to eradicate all types of moral and spiritual evils.
>
> The third level is the conquest of nature. This potential *khalifat Allah* can only be realised through the conquest of nature as exemplified in the *mi'rāj* of our beloved Prophet (pbuh). Nothing, not even the cosmos, could stand in his way in attaining nearness to his Creator. This demonstrates the highest order of *khailifat Allah*.[43]

---

[41] Ansari, *The Qur'ānic Foundations,* vol. 1, 188.

[42] A critique of Communism by Ansari reinforces the materialistic outlook of these ideological systems. Cf. Ansari, *Islam to the Modern Mind,* 204-10.

[43] Ibid., 25-6.

CONCLUSION

Tawhid in a broader sense provides a trajectory for achieving the comprehensive goal as envisaged in the Qur'ān. According to Ansari, "[it] is the only goal to which the pursuit of all the partial goals should bear reference harmonising every of them with the ultimate goals."[44]

---

[44] Ansari, *The Qur'ānic Foundations*, vol. i, 189.